DOMINOE

Moby-Dick

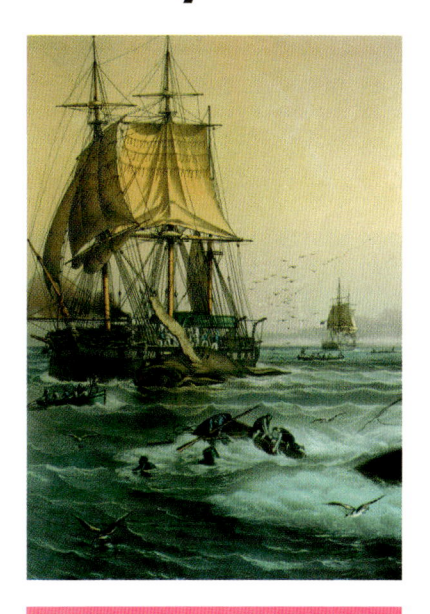

STARTER LEVEL   250 HEADWORDS

OXFORD
UNIVERSITY PRESS

Great Clarendon Street, Oxford, OX2 6DP, United Kingdom

Oxford University Press is a department of the University of Oxford.
It furthers the University's objective of excellence in research, scholarship,
and education by publishing worldwide. Oxford is a registered trade
mark of Oxford University Press in the UK and in certain other countries

This edition © Oxford University Press 2014

The moral rights of the author have been asserted

First published in 2014

2018 2017 2016 2015 2014

10 9 8 7 6 5 4 3 2 1

No unauthorized photocopying

All rights reserved. No part of this publication may be reproduced, stored
in a retrieval system, or transmitted, in any form or by any means, without
the prior permission in writing of Oxford University Press, or as expressly
permitted by law, by licence or under terms agreed with the appropriate
reprographics rights organization. Enquiries concerning reproduction outside
the scope of the above should be sent to the ELT Rights Department, Oxford
University Press, at the address above

You must not circulate this work in any other form and you must impose
this same condition on any acquirer

Links to third party websites are provided by Oxford in good faith and for
information only. Oxford disclaims any responsibility for the materials
contained in any third party website referenced in this work

ISBN: 978 0 19 424978 2   Book
ISBN: 978 0 19 424962 1   Book and MultiROM Pack

MultiROM not available separately

Printed in China

This book is printed on paper from certified and well-managed sources

ACKNOWLEDGEMENTS

Cover image: The Art Archive (whaling/Naval Museum Genoa/Collection Dagli Orti).

Illustrations by: Gianluca Garofalo

The publisher would like to thank the following for permission to reproduce photographs:
Alamy Images p.19 (Whaling ship/The Art Archive); Bridgeman Art Library Ltd
pp.31 (A Shoal of Sperm Whale, engraved by J. Hill, published 1838/© Peabody
Essex Museum, Salem, Massachusetts, USA), 38 (Whaling scrimshaw
(tooth), American School, (18th century)/Private Collection/Photo © Boltin
Picture Library); Corbis pp.40 (Sperm whale/Denis Scott), 41 (Blue whale/
Denis Scott); Getty Images p.18 (Harpoon/Dorling Kindersley); Shutterstock
p.39 (Coffin/3drenderings).

DOMINOES

Series Editors: Bill Bowler and Sue Parminter

Moby-Dick
Herman Melville

Text adaptation by Lesley Thompson
Illustrated by Gianluca Garofalo

Herman Melville (1819–1891) was an American writer from New York. When he was a young man, he worked as a teacher and as a sailor. Many of his early experiences on whaling ships, and living on a South Pacific island, appear in his books. His first novel *Typee* was a sea adventure story. It was very successful when it was published in 1846, and it made Melville famous overnight. His best-known novel, *Moby-Dick*, came out in 1851. The story of Captain Ahab and his hunt for the white whale has been filmed many times.

OXFORD
UNIVERSITY PRESS

ACTIVITIES

BEFORE READING

1 Match the words and pictures. Use a dictionary and look at the story to help you.

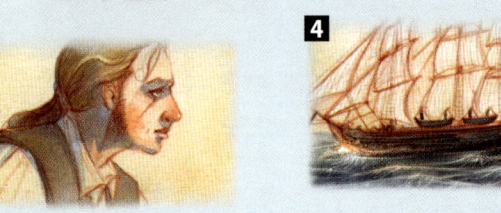

- a ☐ whale
- b ☐ sailor
- c ☐ captain
- d ☐ harpooner
- e ☐ ship
- f ☐ ocean
- g ☐ mate

2 What do you think happens in the story? Complete the sentences with the words from Activity 1.

- a Ishmael, a young American ...., comes from New York.
- b He wants to go to sea, and kill a ....
- c One night, he makes a friend called Queequeg. Queequeg is a ....
- d Ishmael and Queequeg hear of a ...., the *Pequod*, in Nantucket.
- e They want to go and meet Ahab, the .... of the *Pequod*.
- f Starbuck, the first .... on Ahab's ship says, 'We're looking for sailors.'
- g Ishmael and his friend go across the Atlantic .... on the *Pequod*.

CHAPTER 1
Ishmael goes to sea

'Call me Ishmael,' the young American says when he begins his story on the Rachel...

It is 1845, in the **port** of Bedford. Bedford is in North America, near the Atlantic **Ocean**. Ishmael is from New York. He is interested in **whales**. He wants to **sail** the sea, and learn more about them. So he goes to Bedford, and looks for **whaling** work there.

But there are no whaling **ships** in Bedford **harbor** that day. Ishmael must stay the night in Bedford, and look again the next day. He walks through the streets. It is a cold evening. Where can he sleep?

Near the harbor, he finds an old **inn**. He goes in, and speaks to the **landlord**, Peter Coffin. 'I'm a sailor, and new in town. I'd like a room for the night.'

port a town near the sea where ships can stop

ocean a big sea

whale a very big animal that lives in the sea and looks like a fish

sail to go across the water

whaling when you kill whales; for killing whales

ship you use a ship to go across the water

harbor ships stop here

inn an old name for a hotel

landlord this man has an inn, and works there

empty with nobody, or nothing, in it

harpoon people kill whales with this long, thin thing

The landlord says, 'Hmm. I don't have any **empty** rooms tonight, but you can stay in Queequeg's room. He's out now. But he's a sailor, too.'

'OK,' Ishmael says. He gives money to Mr Coffin for the night. The landlord takes him up to Queequeg's room, and leaves him there.

Ishmael is tired. He goes to bed at once. Soon he is sleeping. Later that night, he hears a noise. He sits up suddenly in bed. There is a big man in the room with a **harpoon** in his hand.

'Who are you? And what are you doing with that harpoon? Help!' Ishmael cries.

The landlord comes to the door of the room. 'This is Queequeg. He always has that harpoon with him because he's a harpooner!' Peter Coffin laughs. 'Don't be afraid of him. He's OK.'

There is only one bed in the room. Ishmael sleeps in it that night with Queequeg. But Queequeg is a big man, and there isn't much of the bed for Ishmael.

At breakfast the next morning, Queequeg and Ishmael talk. They laugh about the night before.

'I come from Kokovok, in the South Pacific,' Queequeg says. 'One day I want to go back to my people, and help them. But for now, I'm a whaler. You and I are brothers now,' he smiles. Ishmael is happy with his new friend.

They leave the inn, and visit Bedford harbor. But again there are no whaling ships. Then an old sailor sees Queequeg's harpoon. 'Are you two looking for whaling work?' he asks.

captain the most important person on a ship

strange not usual

on board on, or onto, a ship

mate one of the most important people on a ship after the captain

friendly nice and open with people

'Yes,' they answer.

'Then go to Nantucket – the nearest big port. The *Pequod* is there this week. She's a whaling ship, and her **captain**'s looking for sailors.'

'What's his name?' Ishmael asks.

'Ahab,' the sailor answers. 'He's a good captain, and a good harpooner. But he's a **strange** man.'

'Let's go to Nantucket tomorrow,' Queequeg tells Ishmael.

The next day, they sail to Nantucket. The *Pequod* is in the harbor there. They go **on board**, but they cannot see Captain Ahab. So they speak to Starbuck. Starbuck is the *Pequod*'s first **mate**. He is a **friendly** man.

'My friend Queequeg and I are looking for whaling work,' Ishmael says.

'That's good. Because we're looking for sailors,' Starbuck tells him. 'Young man, can you **row**?'

row to move a boat through water using long pieces of wood

'Yes,' Ishmael answers.

'Good,' Starbuck says. 'We have four whaling **boats** on the *Pequod*. Three boats have a mate, four rowers, and a harpooner. The fourth boat is for Captain Ahab. You can be a rower in my boat, Ishmael. And I need a new harpooner, Queequeg. This man is one of our harpooners, too. Tashtego, meet Queequeg.'

Tashtego is a tall man with long, black hair. He says hello to Queequeg.

The next day, the sailors' families come and say goodbye. The *Pequod* is leaving Nantucket. She's going to sea for four years. So the sailors' families are **sad**.

Ishmael isn't sad. He's excited. But he has many questions in his head: 'Where is Captain Ahab? Is he in his **cabin**? And when is he going to come and speak to his men?'

boat a little ship
sad not happy
cabin a room on a ship

ACTIVITIES

READING CHECK

Match the people in Chapter 1 with the sentences. You can use some names more than once.

Ishmael   Queequeg   Captain Ahab   Peter Coffin   Tashtego   Starbuck

a *Queequeg* comes from Kokovok in the South Pacific.
b .... laughs when Ishmael is afraid of Queequeg.
c An old sailor tells .... and .... about the *Pequod*.
d .... gives work to Ishmael and his friend.
e They meet ...., a tall man with long, black hair.
f Ishmael cannot see .... on the *Pequod* in Nantucket.
g .... is excited and happy when the *Pequod* goes to sea.

WORD WORK

1 Find words from Chapter 1 to match the pictures.

a *boat*
b _ _ _ _ _ _ 
c _ _ _ _ _ _ _ 
d _ _ _ 
e _ _ _ 
f _ _ _ _ _ _ _ _

ACTIVITIES

2 Use the words in the whale to complete the sentences.

Words in whale: strange, port, on board, sail, friendly, empty, mate

a There are many sailors in Bedford because it is a ..... port ....
b There are no .... rooms that night at the inn.
c Mr Starbuck is a nice, ... man.
d Starbuck is the first .... on the *Pequod*.
e Ahab is a good captain, but he is a cold, ... man.
f When Ishmael first goes .... the *Pequod*, he does not see Ahab.
g Ishmael wants to .... the sea and look for whales.

GUESS WHAT

What happens in the next chapter? Tick two boxes to finish each sentence.

1 Ishmael…
    a ☐ sees Captain Ahab.
    b ☐ learns more about the captain.
    c ☐ kills a whale.

2 Captain Ahab…
    a ☐ talks about Moby-Dick.
    b ☐ kills Starbuck.
    c ☐ goes out in a boat.

CHAPTER 2
Ishmael's first whale-hunt

deck where you walk on a ship; ships have two or more of these, one under the other

scar a mark on your body from an old cut

bone a hard, white thing in the body

crew all the people who work on a ship

gold an expensive yellow metal

coin metal money

After a week at sea, Captain Ahab comes on **deck**. He is a tall, old man. He has cold eyes, and a **scar** on his face. All the sailors on the *Pequod* are afraid of him.

'Look at his leg,' Ishmael tells Queequeg. 'It's a whale's **bone**! And his face is angry. Why?'

'Call the **crew** on deck,' Ahab quickly says to Starbuck, the first mate.

Ahab smiles at the sailors when they arrive. He has a **gold coin** in his hand.

'Look, men! See Moby-Dick – the white whale – first, and this coin is for you! I **hate** that white **monster**, and I want his **life**!'

'Captain,' Starbuck says, 'how can you hate an old whale? It's not right!'

'See this whalebone leg, Mr Starbuck!' Ahab answers. 'Moby-Dick must die for that. Are you with me, men?'

'Yes!' the sailors cry.

'Captain,' Starbuck says, 'our work is **hunting** whales, not looking for **revenge**. And the oceans are big. How can we find one whale in all that water?'

'We can, Mr Starbuck,' Ahab says coldly. 'That white monster can't always run away from me. Twenty years is a long time, but I want revenge.'

hate not to like

monster someone or something that does bad things, or that is bad to look at

life what you live

hunt to look for and kill animals; when you look for and kill animals; to look for someone or something

revenge when you do something bad to someone after they do something bad to you

knife (plural **knives**) you cut things with this

That evening, Ishmael asks an older sailor about Moby-Dick. The old man tells the story:

It's 1825, and we're near Japan. We're hunting the white whale with Captain Ahab.

Moby-Dick is under the sea near our boat. We can't see him, but we're waiting quietly for him.

Suddenly, our boat moves up. Moby-Dick is coming up under us! Some men cry out. Soon we're all in the water.

Ahab isn't afraid. He gets on the whale's back with a **knife** in his hand. He brings the knife down into the whale's body many times. 'Die, Moby-Dick, you monster!' he cries.

The white whale looks at Ahab. He takes Ahab's leg angrily in his mouth. Then he closes his mouth on it. The captain can't stop him. Soon after, we bring Ahab back to our ship. We take him to his cabin, and we put him on his bed. 'Moby-Dick has my leg!' he cries. 'He must die for this!' From that day, Captain Ahab's life changes. Now he never stops thinking of Moby-Dick. He wants revenge!

Late the next day, Ishmael sees his first whale-hunt. Tashtego is up on the **mast**, and he cries, 'Look! Whales!'

The men run to their boats. But what is this? Five strange men in black **clothes** are helping Captain Ahab into his boat, too.

'Good for him!' the second mate laughs. 'Four boats are better than three!'

Starbuck says nothing. After Ahab's talk of revenge, the first mate is not happy about this evening's whale-hunt.

Soon the boats are rowing fast after the whales. The fastest boat of all has Ahab in it.

Ishmael and Queequeg are in Starbuck's boat. The sky is dark now. They hear a whale near them, but they cannot see it. Suddenly Queequeg stands up. He **throws** his harpoon at the whale, but he does not kill it. The whale hits the boat angrily with its **tail**. After that, Starbuck's boat begins to go down. They can't row back to the *Pequod* now. Just then, somebody in the boat cries, 'Oh, no! Look!'

The *Pequod* is coming right at them. She's going to hit them!

mast a tall thing on an old ship where someone sits and looks out

clothes people wear these

throw to move something through the air with your hand and arm

tail the long thing at the back of an animal's body

11

ACTIVITIES

READING CHECK

Are these sentences true or false? Tick the boxes.   True   False

- **a** Ahab wants to kill Moby-Dick.
- **b** Moby-Dick has Ahab's arm.
- **c** Ahab wants to give money to his men for finding Moby-Dick.
- **d** Starbuck wants to find and kill Moby-Dick.
- **e** Ahab has a boat, and ten strange sailors.
- **f** Queequeg does not kill the whale.
- **g** The whale hits Starbuck's boat.
- **h** Starbuck's boat can go back to the *Pequod*.

WORD WORK

Correct the sentences about the pictures with words from Chapter 2.

a Some people have a long ~~knife~~. *life*

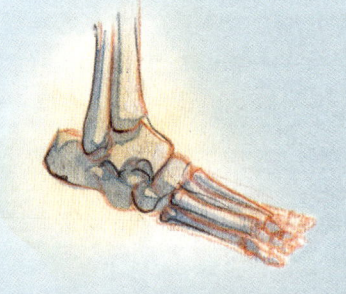

b There are a lot of *phones* in a man's foot.

c This *coat* is very old.

ACTIVITIES

d Be careful! That man has a *life* in his hand.

e She is wearing beautiful *clocks*.

f My cat's *table* is very long.

GUESS WHAT

What happens in the next chapter? Choose the words to complete the sentences.

a Starbuck's men are all *alive / dead*.
b Tashtego sees something *black / white* in the water.
c The men are *happy / not happy* after they kill a whale.
d Ahab is *interested / not interested* in his men's work.
e Tashtego falls into the *sea / captain's boat*.
f Ishmael wants to *kill / help* Tashtego.

13

CHAPTER 3
Something terrible in the ocean

'Into the water, men! Fast!' Starbuck cries. At once, all the sailors from his boat **jump** into the ocean. Seconds later, the *Pequod* goes over their boat. But Starbuck is happy because all his men are alive. They **swim** quickly over to the ship, and go on board.

After that, the ship sails down to the south of Africa. The crew of Ahab's boat come out on deck then. All of them are wearing black clothes. Their **master** is Fedallah. He makes no noise when he moves **around** the ship. He always talks quietly to his men. He often walks on the deck of the *Pequod* with Ahab. And when they are walking, he speaks quietly in the captain's ear. But he never talks to any of the ship's crew.

jump to move quickly from one thing to a different thing

swim to go through the water moving your body

master the most important man; he tells people to do things

around to different places on something; all the way round

Ishmael is afraid of Fedallah. The sailors tell strange stories about him. Fedallah can see into the **future**, some of them say.

One afternoon, Tashtego is up on the mast. Suddenly, the men down on the deck hear his cry. 'Look! There's something big and white in the water! It's Moby-Dick!'

'Into the boats, men,' Ahab cries to the crew. 'Remember that gold coin!'

But when the boats arrive at the white thing, they find no whale. It is something more **terrible** – a **giant** white **squid**. Its many arms are moving around with the water. But the squid is dead.

'What a strange thing!' Starbuck says. 'Giant squid usually live far down under the ocean, and whales eat them. This is bad **luck** for us all, I feel.'

'No, Mr Starbuck! You're wrong,' says Queequeg. 'It's good luck. When you see a giant squid, whales are never far away. Wait and see.'

future the time that is coming

terrible very bad

giant very big

squid (*plural* **squid**) a long thin sea animal with eight arms

luck when things happen to you that are very good, or very bad

Queequeg is right. The next day, the men hunt and kill a big blue whale. They take its dead body back to the ship. They are very happy. Now they have a lot of whale **oil** for their **barrels**. They work on the dead whale's body with their knives. And for many hours they sing happily at their work.

But Ahab isn't happy. He looks coldly at the dead, blue whale, and he says nothing. Then he goes back to his cabin, and he closes the door behind him.

'Ahab isn't interested in the oil,' Starbuck thinks. 'He wants a bigger whale – a white whale. He wants Moby-Dick! He needs revenge!'

The men work on the dead whale all day. It is on the **ropes** at the front of the *Pequod*. The sailors carefully put the expensive oil from the whale's body into many barrels on deck. But in the afternoon something terrible happens. Tashtego has oil on his hands. He **falls** from one of the ropes down into the whale's empty head.

oil a liquid that comes from whales; people use it in lights

barrel a tall round box; you can put oil or water in it

rope you put this around your body when you climb a tree or something very high

fall to go down suddenly

Then the giant head falls from the whale's body, and into the ocean. Tashtego goes with it. And the whale's head, with Tashtego in it, goes down under the water. Queequeg quickly jumps into the sea after his friend.

Minutes later, Starbuck's boat is in the water, too. It is going to help them. Ishmael is one of the rowers on the boat. He cannot see Queequeg now because he is under the water. 'Oh no! Is my good friend dead?' he thinks sadly.

ACTIVITIES

READING CHECK

Put these sentences in order. Number them 1–8.

- **a** ☐ Tashtego falls into the whale's head, and then into the sea.
- **b** ☐ The crew find a dead squid in the water.
- **c** ☐ Queequeg jumps into the sea after Tashtego.
- **d** ☐ The *Pequod* goes over Starbuck's boat.
- **e** ☐ The sailors work on the dead whale with their knives.
- **f** ☐ Tashtego sees something white in the sea.
- **g** ☐ Fedallah and his crew come out on deck.
- **h** ☐ The men kill a big blue whale.

WORD WORK

1 Find words from Chapter 3 in the harpoon.

ropeswimaroundfutureterriblesquidluckoilfall

ACTIVITIES

2 Complete the sentences with the words from Activity 1 on page 18.

- **a** In the ....*future*...., I want to be a writer.
- **b** That boy is only five, but he can .... 100 meters.
- **c** My brothers like to run .... in the garden all day.
- **d** 'I'm looking for work.' 'Good ....!'
- **e** Some whale .... is very expensive.
- **f** Be careful! Don't .... from that tree!
- **g** There are a lot of .... in the Mediterranean Sea.
- **h** It's cold, and it's raining. What a .... night!
- **i** He can't run away because there is a .... around his legs.

GUESS WHAT

What happens in the next chapter? Tick two boxes.

- **a** ☐ Queequeg pulls Tashtego out of the whale's head.
- **b** ☐ Tashtego and Queequeg die in the sea.
- **c** ☐ Ahab talks to an English captain about Moby-Dick.
- **d** ☐ Starbuck leaves the *Pequod* and goes home with his men.

CHAPTER 4
Let's forget Moby-Dick

Ishmael's friend Queequeg is swimming down to the whale's head. It is falling slowly to the ocean bed. Can Queequeg **pull** Tashtego out of it in time?

The men on the *Pequod* cannot see through the dark water. They watch from the deck, and wait. Nobody speaks. After some minutes, Queequeg's head comes up out of the water. He is pulling Tashtego behind him – and he is alive! Ishmael helps them on board Starbuck's boat. And soon they are back on the ship again.

'Good work, Queequeg,' Starbuck smiles. '**Maybe** our luck is changing after all.'

pull to move something nearer you

maybe perhaps

But is Starbuck right? In the Indian Ocean, they find no whales. Where are they all?

'Maybe there aren't any more whales in the sea,' Ishmael thinks, 'after all the hunting.'

Nothing happens for days after this, and Ahab stays in his cabin. Then the sailors suddenly see many whales in front of them. Is their luck changing?

The whaling boats go out. Soon there are whales all around them.

'Be careful, boys! Watch their tails!' Starbuck cries. 'There are young whales here, and their mothers don't want whalers near them!'

After many hours, the boats go back to the *Pequod*. They have only one whale with them, and it is not very big. 'Our work is never easy,' Starbuck thinks tiredly.

Then Ahab sees a ship not far away. It is the *Samuel Enderby*. He calls out to the English captain, 'I'm looking for a giant white whale! Can you help me?'

Captain Boomer answers, 'Yes, I can. Look!' He puts up his arm. It is a whale's bone.

Ahab is excited. 'Take me over to the *Samuel Enderby* – quickly!' he says to his men.

'Ahab's going **crazy**,' Starbuck thinks.

On board the *Samuel Enderby*, Ahab says hello. He hits his whalebone leg, and Captain Boomer's whalebone arm, with his hand. Boomer laughs. He is a friendly man, and his face is red from the sun.

'Tell me more about this white whale,' Ahab says.

'Oh, I remember him well,' Boomer answers. 'He has a giant head, and scars all over his body. There's an old harpoon in his back –'

'That's my harpoon!' Ahab cries. 'So it is him – Moby-Dick! Where is he now?'

crazy not thinking well

'I don't know. I'm talking about last year, but I can see it all in my head. First, he **breaks** my boat in two with his tail. Before I know it, I'm in the sea. Suddenly he pulls me under the water. Then the harpoon in his back goes into my arm. It comes out near my hand. After that, my first mate pulls me from the water, and takes me to my ship. I stay for weeks in my bed, and my arm goes black. In the end, the ship's **carpenter cuts off** my arm with his knife – a terrible thing! So I lose my arm, but I'm alive. That's something!'

'And the white whale?' Ahab asks.

'Ah, he's out there, the old monster! He has my arm, but he can't have any more of me!' Boomer laughs. 'And he has your leg, too, Captain Ahab. So let's forget Moby-Dick, I say! What about you?'

break to make one thing into two or more things when you hit it

carpenter this person makes things like tables and chairs

cut off to take a little thing away from a bigger thing with a knife

ACTIVITIES

READING CHECK

Choose the correct words to complete the sentences.

a When Tashtego is under the water, nobody *speaks* / *drinks*.
b The men on the *Pequod* don't see many *ships* / *whales* in the Indian Ocean.
c Ahab stays in his *cabin* / *port* for many days.
d The men kill one *little* / *giant* whale.
e The captain of the *Samuel Enderby* has a whalebone *leg* / *arm*.
f Ahab is interested in *Captain Boomer* / *the white whale*.
g Captain Boomer *wants* / *does not want* to see Moby-Dick again.
h Ahab's *harpoon* / *knife* is in Moby-Dick's back.

WORD WORK

1 Find words from Chapter 4 in the barrels.

YAMEB   LULP   KAREB

a maybe   b ....   c ....

RENTEPRAC   ZARYC   TUC FOF

d ....   e ....   f ....

ACTIVITIES

2 Complete the sentences with the words from Activity 1 on page 24.

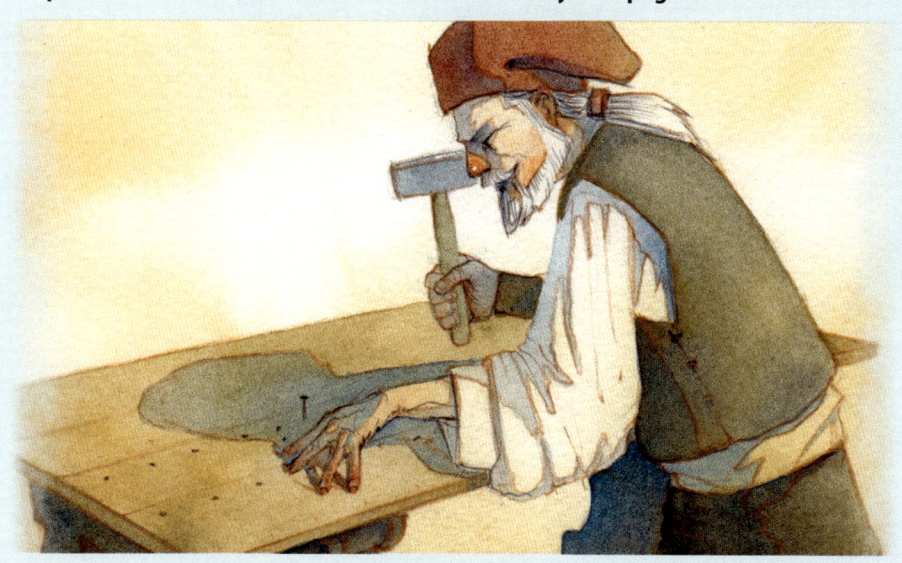

a The ..carpenter.. is making a nice, new table for me.
b Hmm. I don't know. .... I can see you later.
c What a strange man. Is he ...., do you think?
d Be careful! That's my best chair. Please don't .... it.
e 'I'm sorry, Captain Boomer, but I must .... this arm or you're going to die,' says the carpenter.
f Hey! That girl can't swim. Quick! .... her out of the water!

GUESS WHAT

What happens in the next chapter? Tick the boxes.   Yes   No

a Ahab goes back to the *Pequod*.
b Ahab forgets all about Moby-Dick.
c The *Pequod* sails back to America.
d Starbuck tells Ahab something bad about the ship.
e Ahab is interested when Starbuck speaks to him.
f Queequeg is very ill.
g Ahab dies in his cabin.
h Captain Gardiner, an old friend of Ahab's, asks for his help.

CHAPTER 5
Can you help me, Ahab?

'Forget Moby-Dick? Never!' Ahab cries. 'I want to have my revenge!'

Boomer looks at Ahab strangely. 'What's the matter with you, Captain? Moby-Dick's a whale, not a man. Why are you looking for revenge on him? Are you crazy?'

'Question me no more!' Ahab says, angrily. 'Take me back to the *Pequod*!' he tells his men. 'The white whale is calling! I must go!'

Some weeks later, the *Pequod* is near Japan. Ahab is very excited. Moby-Dick is not far away, he feels! One evening, Starbuck visits Ahab's cabin. 'There's oil on one of the decks, Captain,' he says. 'It's coming from the barrels. We can't lose it. We must bring the barrels up, and look for **holes** in them.'

'The whale oil doesn't matter!' Ahab cries.

'Captain!' Starbuck says. 'I'm asking you for the last time. Forget the white whale. Think about your men!'

'Are you asking, or telling me?' Ahab says. He takes his **gun** in his hand, and looks at Starbuck. 'There's only one captain on this ship. Remember that!'

hole an opening in something

gun a person can kill someone with this

'Yes, Captain,' Starbuck answers him. At the same time, he is thinking, 'But maybe soon I must kill you, you crazy old man.'

Ahab puts his gun down. 'All right, Starbuck. Go and look at those barrels,' he says. 'I'm not interested.'

Hours later, there are barrels all over the deck. Queequeg looks carefully at them all. In the end, he finds a hole in one of them. He puts the oil from it into a new barrel. But he is cold after this work late at night, and the next day he is very ill. 'I'm dying,' he tells Ishmael. 'Bring the ship's carpenter here. He must make a **coffin** for me. And bring my harpoon, too.'

Ishmael is sorry for his friend. He goes for the carpenter.

The carpenter comes and makes a big coffin. Queequeg gets in it with his harpoon. 'It's a good coffin,' he says.

But after three days, Queequeg is well again. 'I can't die now,' he says. 'The time isn't right. And later I must go home and help my people. The coffin can wait.'

Ishmael is happy for his friend.

One night, Captain Ahab has a terrible dream. In this **dream**, he dies at sea. 'Can it be true?' he asks Fedallah.

coffin a box that you put a dead person's body in

dream a picture that you see in your head when you are sleeping

27

Fedallah looks into the future. Then he says, 'Before you can die, you must see two coffins on the sea. One is alive, and one is of **wood**. A rope is going to kill you, Master. But I'm going to die first!'

The sky is black with rain now. But Ahab laughs at the rain, and at the white **lightning** in the sky. 'You cannot kill me,' he cries. 'This scar on my face is your work – but look at me – I live!'

wood the hard part of a tree

lightning the light in the sky when there is a storm

Just then, there is a cry from the mast, and a sailor falls into the sea. 'More bad luck, Captain,' Starbuck says. 'Let's go home!' But Ahab is not listening.

Later that day, a big whaling ship – the *Rachel* – arrives near the *Pequod*. Captain Gardiner of the *Rachel* knows Ahab well.

'Can you help me, Ahab?' Gardiner calls across the sea. 'We can't find one of our boats, and my young son's on it.'

Starbuck looks at Ahab. Is the captain listening to his old friend? Can he forget for one minute about Moby-Dick?

ACTIVITIES

READING CHECK

Choose the best answer for each question.

a What does Ahab want?
   1 ☐ Money.
   2 ☐ Love.
   3 ☑ Revenge.

b What does Starbuck tell Ahab?
   1 ☐ 'Moby-Dick is dead.'
   2 ☐ 'Oil is coming out of the barrels.'
   3 ☐ 'Captain Boomer is crazy.'

c Why is Starbuck angry with Ahab?
   1 ☐ Ahab is interested in Moby-Dick.
   2 ☐ Ahab sleeps all the time.
   3 ☐ Ahab kills people.

d What does Starbuck think about Ahab?
   1 ☐ He is old.
   2 ☐ He is nice.
   3 ☐ He is crazy.

e Why is Queequeg ill?
   1 ☐ He doesn't eat well.
   2 ☐ He works for many hours in the cold night.
   3 ☐ He falls into the cold sea.

f What does Fedallah say to Ahab?
   1 ☐ 'You're going to die.'
   2 ☐ 'You're going to kill Starbuck.'
   3 ☐ 'You're going to kill Ishmael.'

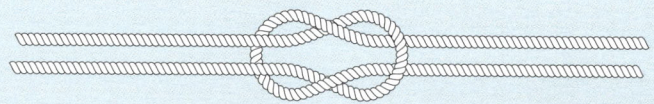

WORD WORK

Read the sentences and complete the puzzle on page 31 with words from Chapter 5.

a Tables and chairs are often made of ..... wood ....
b .... sometimes comes from the sky and hits buildings, trees, or people.
c When someone dies, we put their body in a ....
d In a .... you can often do strange things.
e I'm making a .... in the garden because I want to put a new tree in it.
f A knife or a .... can kill people.

ACTIVITIES

GUESS WHAT

How does the story finish? Tick one box.

a ☐ Starbuck and his men kill Ahab.
b ☐ Moby-Dick and all the men die.
c ☐ Ahab kills Moby-Dick.
d ☐ Moby-Dick and Ishmael live, but Ahab dies.

31

CHAPTER 6
Revenge!

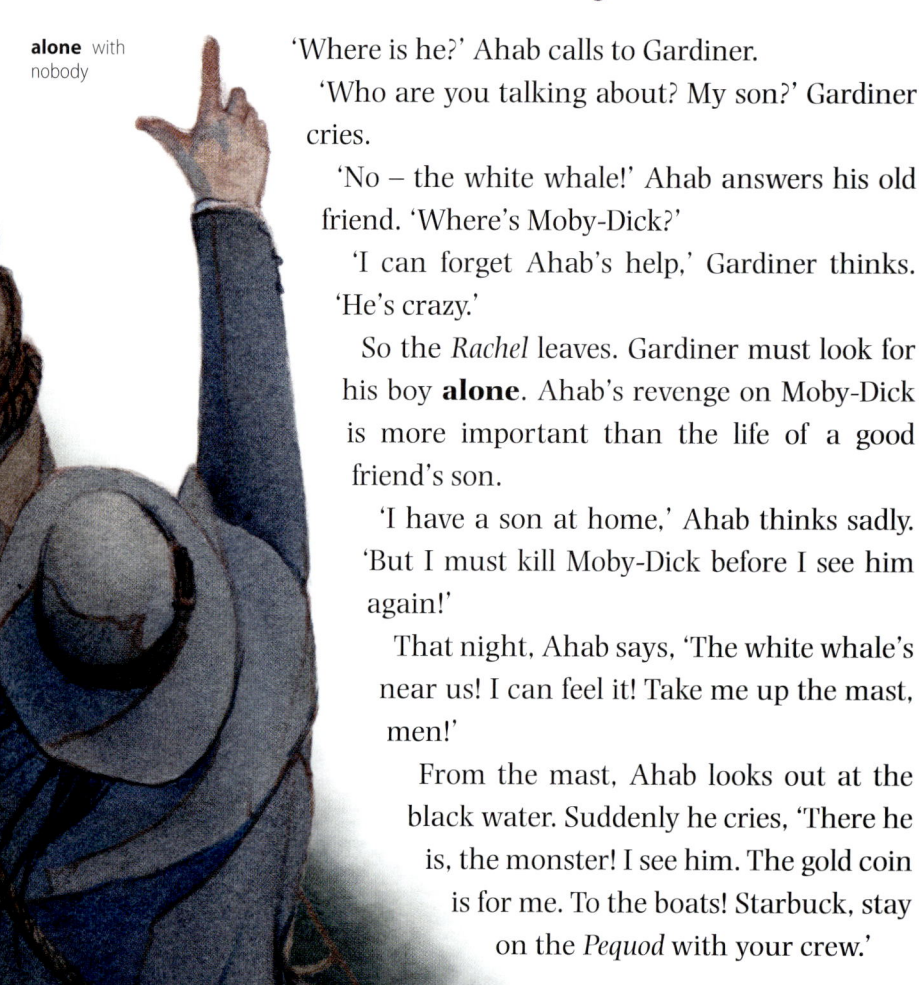

alone with nobody

'Where is he?' Ahab calls to Gardiner.

'Who are you talking about? My son?' Gardiner cries.

'No – the white whale!' Ahab answers his old friend. 'Where's Moby-Dick?'

'I can forget Ahab's help,' Gardiner thinks. 'He's crazy.'

So the *Rachel* leaves. Gardiner must look for his boy **alone**. Ahab's revenge on Moby-Dick is more important than the life of a good friend's son.

'I have a son at home,' Ahab thinks sadly. 'But I must kill Moby-Dick before I see him again!'

That night, Ahab says, 'The white whale's near us! I can feel it! Take me up the mast, men!'

From the mast, Ahab looks out at the black water. Suddenly he cries, 'There he is, the monster! I see him. The gold coin is for me. To the boats! Starbuck, stay on the *Pequod* with your crew.'

The hunt for Moby-Dick takes three days. On the first day, the whale swims quickly away from their boats.

'Grrr! He's laughing at us,' Ahab says. 'Give the harpoon to me!' Just then, the white whale swims under Ahab's boat. He comes up suddenly, and breaks the boat in two. Starbuck, on the *Pequod*, quickly pulls everyone from the water.

'Listen, men!' Ahab cries on the deck of his ship. 'See the white monster tomorrow, and the gold is for you! I see him first, and I give you all ten times the money! Sleep well tonight. Tomorrow we kill Moby-Dick!'

On day two of the hunt, the white whale swims in front of the ship. He jumps out of the sea again and again. 'This is your last day, you monster,' Ahab says. 'To the boats!'

Ahab and his crew go out in Starbuck's boat. Moby-Dick hits the second and third mates' boats with his tail. The harpooners in them throw their harpoons into his body, but he moves around crazily. Soon all the ropes are **tangled**. The two boats go over, and the men fall into the water. Moby-Dick goes to Ahab last, and hits Starbuck's boat with his head. Soon everyone is in the water. Again, Starbuck pulls them back on board the *Pequod*.

Ahab calls all the crew on deck, but Fedallah is not there with them. 'Ah, my true friend,' Ahab thinks sadly. 'So the sea has you now.'

'Let's stop this crazy hunt, Captain,' Starbuck says. 'The white whale's faster than us. We can never kill him. Forget Moby-Dick!'

'Noooo!' Ahab cries. 'I need revenge! We're going to kill him tomorrow. Then we can go home. Let's ask the crew. Are you with me, men?'

'We are!' all the sailors cry.

tangled having different things together that are not easy to pull apart

On day three, the sky is dark, but the three boats go out again. Soon they find Moby-Dick before them: a giant white hill half under the sea. The men say nothing, but they are afraid. 'Go to him, men. Kill him!' Ahab cries. Then they all see something terrible. Fedallah's dead body is **lying** on the whale. The harpoon ropes from the day before are tangled around the two of them.

'Ah! So Fedallah dies before me, and Moby-Dick's his coffin. Oh, this monster's playing with me!' Ahab says.

Just then, one of the sailors cries, 'Hey, look! The whale's going for the ship!'

Moby-Dick hits the *Pequod* with his big, white head. He makes a hole in her, and she begins to go down.

'Aargh! My ship!' Ahab cries. 'But wait! That's Fedallah's second coffin – the coffin of wood!'

lie to have all of your body on something

Ahab throws his harpoon angrily, and he hits the whale's back. But Moby-Dick is swimming away fast. The harpoon rope goes around Ahab's body, and it pulls him into the ocean. For some minutes, the white whale pulls the captain behind him. At first, Ahab has his head up out of the water. But then the whale goes far down under the sea. So Ahab goes down with him, and he dies. He never has his revenge on Moby-Dick!

The *Pequod* goes down, too – with all her crew. And she takes the three whaling-boats with her. At the last minute, Ishmael jumps into the ocean. He swims away fast. All the sailors from the *Pequod* die, but Ishmael lives. He is happy about that, but where can he go now?

Suddenly, he sees Queequeg's empty coffin on the water. He swims over to it, and he gets on it. For a day and a night, he lies on that coffin – alone in the blue Pacific Ocean.

Ishmael is **lucky**. Two days later, the *Rachel* sails back. Captain Gardiner finds Ishmael lying on the coffin, and takes him on board. Sadly, Gardiner never finds his young son, but luckily he **saves** Ishmael's life.

lucky having something happen that is good for you

save to stop bad things happening to something

> That night, the sailors on the Rachel ask Ishmael for his story. He tells it – for the first of many times. It is the story of Captain Ahab's crazy last days, and of his hunt for the terrible white whale, Moby-Dick!

ACTIVITIES

READING CHECK

Correct the sentences.

a   Captain Gardiner is looking for his ~~daughter~~ *son*.

b   Love is more important to Ahab than his friend's child.

c   Starbuck sees Moby-Dick first.

d   The hunt for Moby-Dick takes five days.

e   Ahab stays on the *Pequod* with the crew.

f   Moby-Dick breaks Ahab's arm in two.

g   Fedallah's harpoon is lying on the whale.

h   The *Pequod* goes down after Moby-Dick's tail hits it.

i   Moby-Dick pulls Queequeg down under the water with him.

j   Ishmael lies on Queequeg's table, and lives.

k   The *Rachel* finds Ishmael two weeks later.

ACTIVITIES

WORD WORK

Complete the sentences with the words in the coffin.

Coffin contains: lucky, save, tangled, ~~lie~~, alone

a You're tired. Why don't you .... *lie* .... down on the bed and sleep?
b Ishmael is .... because Moby-Dick doesn't kill him.
c I don't like being .... I like being with my friends.
d That little girl's hair is all .... and dirty.
e Today, many people want to .... whales, and not kill them.

GUESS WHAT

What happens to Ishmael after the story finishes? Tick the boxes, and add your own ideas.

a ☐ He never goes to sea again.
b ☐ He visits Queequeg's family in the South Pacific.
c ☐ He works at Peter Coffin's inn.
d ☐ He goes back to New York.
e ....
f ....
g ....

PROJECTS

PROJECT A *Different whales*

1 There are many different kinds of whale. Read the text about the sperm whale and complete the information table. Use a dictionary to help you.

> The sperm whale is a big whale. It can be up to 16 meters long. The sperm whale weighs up to 41,000 kilograms, and lives for about 70 years. Sperm whales live in all the world's oceans. Their favourite food is squid – and especially giant squid. Sperm whales can eat squid because they have between thirty and sixty teeth in the lower part of their mouths. Like many whales, sperm whales 'talk' to each other with clicks. These are very noisy!

Kind of whale:	
Length:	
Weighs:	
Lives for:	
Lives in:	
Eats:	
Other interesting information:	

2 Look at the information in the table below, and complete the text about the blue whale on page 41.

Kind of whale:	blue whale
Length:	up to 30 meters long
Weighs:	up to 181,000 kilograms
Lives for:	about 90 years
Lives in:	the Pacific, Antarctic, and Indian Oceans
Eats:	krill (very little sea animals)
Other interesting information:	the biggest animal of all time

PROJECTS

The blue whale is the giant of the seas. It can be up to .... long, and it weighs up to .... Blue whales .... for about .... years. They live in the ...., ..., and .... Oceans. Blue whales do not have teeth, and they eat a lot of .... These are very little ...., and they are easy to eat. The blue whale is the biggest whale of all. In fact, it is the .... of all time!

3 Choose a different whale. Find out about it on the Internet. Make notes about your whale in the table below.

HUMPBACK WHALE **BELUGA**
GRAY WHALE **FIN WHALE**
ORCA WHALE

Kind of whale:	
Length:	
Weighs:	
Lives for:	
Lives in:	
Eats:	
Other interesting information:	

4 Write a short text about your whale. Use your notes, and the texts in Activities 1 and 2, to help you.

PROJECTS

Project B — *Poems in shapes*

Poems often have 'rhymes' in them. A rhyme is when two lines of a poem finish in a word with the same sound at the end – like *old* and *cold*.

Some poems can be in shapes on the page, too.

1 Choose the best words to complete this poem by Starbuck. (Think of the rhymes.) Use a dictionary to help you.

The crew of the *Pequod* are the *nicest / best* –
Young or old, from *East or West / North or South*.
The *Pequod* is our home *at sea / on the ocean*,
And we're all one *big group of friends / family*.
It's exciting *living a sailor's life / doing whaling work*,
But when am I going back home to *my wife / America*?

2 Complete these two story character poems with the words in the boxes. Use a dictionary to help you.

| dreams monster ocean oil revenge sails terrible whales |

a Across the .... the *Pequod* ....
We look for .... , we look for ....
The most .... of them all is white.
I have .... of him eating my leg at night!
.... on Moby-Dick fills my head:
I want that old, white .... dead!

PROJECTS

| barrels | boats | coffins | deck | holes | mast | row | wood |

b I work on the *Pequod*, and I'm good.
I make .... for dead men, and things from .... :
I can make .... for sailors to ....
I can mend .... in old .... , you know.
I can mend a flat .... , or a tall ship's ....
I work well, and I work fast!

3 Match a story character with each poem in Activity 2.

1
2
3
4
5
6
7
8
9
10

43

PROJECTS

4 Choose a story character. Make notes about your character in the table.

| What can / does he do? |
| What does he like / hate doing? |
| Who does he like / hate? |
| What does he want? / What is his dream? |
| What does he feel about his life? |

5 Write a short poem about your character. Put it in a shape (a coin, a barrel, a whaling boat, or a knife maybe). You can use rhymes if you want.

6 Put your finished poem on the classroom wall. Read your classmates' poems. Which do you like best? Why?

GRAMMAR

GRAMMAR CHECK

Information questions and question words

We use question words in information questions.

Where is the port of Bedford?   *Who is the landlord of the inn?*

We answer these questions by giving information.

In North America.   *Peter Coffin.*

We use **what** for things, **where** for places, **who** for people, **why** for reasons, **which** for one of many things, and **how much** / **how many** for quantities. We use **how much** with singular nouns, and **how many** with plural nouns.

How much time does Ishmael have? Not much.   *How many people are at the inn? A lot.*

1 Complete the information questions with the question words in the box.

How many   How much   What   ~~When~~   Where   Which   Who   Why

a Q: ....When.... does Ishmael's story begin?
A: In 1845.

b Q: .... does he come from?
A: New York.

c Q: .... does he go to Bedford?
A: Because he wants to find whaling work.

d Q: .... inn does he stay at?
A: The inn near the harbor.

e Q: .... does Ishmael speak to when he arrives?
A: The landlord.

f Q: .... does Ishmael ask for?
A: A room.

g Q: .... money does he have?
A: Not a lot.

h Q: .... nights does he want to stay?
A: One.

GRAMMAR

GRAMMAR CHECK

There is* and *there are

We use **there is** (**there's**) and **there are** to talk about the things and people in a place.

There's a ship in the harbor.   There are five men in the boat.

To make sentences negative, we use **there is** / **there are** + **not** (**there isn't** / **there aren't**).

There isn't anyone in the room.   There aren't many people on the ship.

In questions, we change the order of **there** and the verb **is** / **are**.

In short answers, we re-use **there** + the verb **be**.

Is there a whale in the harbor? No, there isn't.

Are there any boats in the water? No, there aren't.

We don't use contractions in affirmative short answers.

Yes, there is. ✔   ~~*Yes, there's.*~~ ✘

2 Complete the text with *there is* or *there are* in the correct form (affirmative, question form, or negative).

a) **There aren't** any whaling ships in Bedford harbor. So Ishmael visits Peter Coffin's inn, but b) .... any empty rooms. Ishmael sleeps in Queequeg's room, but suddenly, c) .... a man in the room with him. Luckily it's Queequeg! The next day, an old sailor tells Ishmael and Queequeg, d) '.................. any whaling work in Bedford. Go to Nantucket!' So the two friends go there, and find the *Pequod*. e) '.................. any work for us on your ship?' they ask Starbuck, the first mate. He tells them, 'Well, f) .... four whaling boats on the *Pequod*. And I need a harpooner and a rower on my boat.' The next day, the *Pequod* goes to sea. 'Why g) .... a lot of people in the harbor today?' Ishmael asks. 'They're saying goodbye to us,' Starbuck answers.

3 Write short answers to these questions.

a Are there different mates on the *Pequod*?
   Yes, there are.

b Are there any women on the ship?
   ....

c Is there a carpenter on the ship?
   ....

d Are there different harpooners on the ship?
   ....

e Is there a television on the ship?
   ....

GRAMMAR

GRAMMAR CHECK

Present Simple: *Yes / No* questions and short answers

We use auxiliary verbs and *be* (main verb) in *Yes / No* questions.

Can Ishmael row? (can + subject + infinitive without *to*)

Does he like Queequeg? (do + subject + infinitive without *to*)

Is Queequeg American? (be + subject)

In the short answer, we re-use the auxiliary verb or *be* (main verb).

Yes, he can.   Yes, he does.   No, he isn't (= is not).

4 Write answers for the questions about Captain Ahab. Use the short answers in the box.

> No, he can't.   No, he doesn't.   No, he isn't.   Yes, he can.   Yes, he does.
> ~~Yes, he does.~~   Yes, he is.   Yes, it is.   Yes, they are.

a Does Ahab come from America?
...........Yes, he does...........

b Is he a happy man?
....

c Can he forget Moby-Dick?
....

d Can he throw a harpoon?
....

e Does he often talk to Ishmael?
....

f Does Ahab have a scar on his face?
....

g Is one of his legs a whale's bone?
....

h Are his eyes cold?
....

i Is he crazy in the end?
....

GRAMMAR

GRAMMAR CHECK

Present Simple: third person –s

We can use the Present Simple to tell a story very dramatically.

We add –s to the infinitive without to to make the third person *(he / she / it)* form of the Present Simple.

Starbuck says goodbye to his family.

When verbs end in *–o*, *–ch*, *–ss*, or *–sh*, we add *–es* to make the third person form.

go – He goes on board the Pequod.

When verbs end in consonant + *–y*, we change the *y* to *i*, and add *–es*.

cry – He cries, 'The captain wants all the crew on deck!'

The verbs *be* and *have* are irregular.

Starbuck has a friendly face.   He isn't (= is not) interested in revenge.

5 Complete the text about Ahab and Moby-Dick with the verbs in brackets in the Present Simple.

In 1825, Ahab **a)** ....*is*.... (be) near Japan. He **b)** .... (see) the white whale, Moby-Dick, in the water, and he **c)** .... (want) to kill him. Ahab **d)** .... (have) his knife with him. Moby-Dick **e)** .... (swim) under Ahab's boat. Suddenly, the boat **f)** .... (move) up, and all the men in it cry out. Ahab **g)** .... (not be) afraid. He **h)** .... (take) his knife, and he **i)** .... (bring) it down on the whale's body. 'Die, Moby-Dick!' he **j)** .... (cry). The white whale **k)** .... (close) his mouth on Ahab's leg. Ahab can do nothing.
From that day, Ahab's life **l)** .... (change). He **m)** .... (go) to many countries, and he **n)** .... (kill) many whales. But he never **o)** .... (stop) thinking about Moby-Dick.

GRAMMAR

GRAMMAR CHECK

Possessive 's and s'

We use possessive 's and s' to show that something belongs to someone or something.

When the person or thing is singular, we use 's.

Tashtego's hair is black.   The dead squid's arms are moving.

When the people or things are plural, we use s'.

The sailors' families are saying goodbye.   The young whales' mothers are with them.

With irregular plural nouns, we use 's.

The men's work isn't easy.   The children's faces are sad.

6 Rewrite the sentences using the possessive 's or s'.

a The whaling crew of Ahab are strange men.
   Ahab's whaling crew are strange men.

b The dreams of Fedallah are interesting.
   ....

c The clothes of his men are black.
   ....

d The stories of sailors are interesting.
   ....

e The mast of the *Pequod* is tall.
   ....

f The eyes of the mother whales are angry.
   ....
   ....

g The cries of their children are terrible.
   ....
   ....

h The life of Ishmael is exciting.
   ....
   ....

GRAMMAR

GRAMMAR CHECK

Linkers: *and*, *but*, *so*, and *because*

and links two parts of a sentence with the same idea.

Captain Boomer is friendly, and he laughs a lot.

but links two parts of a sentence with different ideas.

Boomer wants to forget Moby-Dick, but Ahab wants revenge.

so links two parts of a sentence talking about the result of something.

Captain Boomer's arm goes bad, so they cut it off.

(= result of first part of sentence)

because links two parts of a sentence talking about the reason for something.

Ahab cries out angrily because Moby-Dick has his leg.

(= reason for first part of sentence)

We usually put a comma before **and**, **but**, and **so** in the middle of a sentence.

7 Complete the sentences with *and*, *but*, *so*, or *because*.

a Tashtego is working happily, ...**but**...... he hits his head on the mast.
b He falls into the whale's empty head, ... it falls off the deck.
c Queequeg wants to save Tashtego, ... he jumps into the sea.
d Starbuck gets into his boat .... he wants to help, too.
e Ishmael goes with Starbuck, ... he rows Starbuck's boat.
f Ishmael looks for Queequeg, ... he can't see him.
g The men on the *Pequod* say nothing .... they are afraid.
h Tashtego can't get out of the head, ... he goes down with it.
i It isn't very easy, ... Queequeg pulls Tashtego out.
j He brings Tashtego up, ... Tashtego is alive!

50

GRAMMAR

GRAMMAR CHECK

Prepositions of movement

Prepositions of movement tell us how something moves.

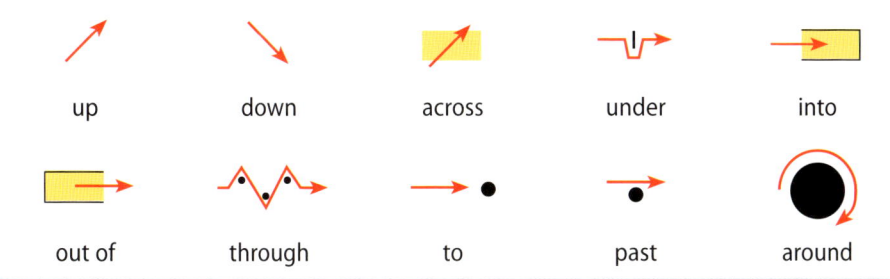

up	down	across	under	into
out of	through	to	past	around

8 Complete the text about the hunt for Moby-Dick with the prepositions in the box.

> across around around down into into out of
> past ~~through~~ to to under under up

On day one of the hunt, Moby-Dick swims away **a)** ...through... the water fast. Ahab takes a harpoon in his hand. But Moby-Dick swims **b)** .... Ahab's boat. He comes **c)** .... suddenly, and breaks it. Starbuck, on the *Pequod*, pulls everyone **d)** .... the water. On day two, the men hit Moby-Dick with their harpoons, but he moves his tail **e)** .... crazily. The boats break, and the sailors fall **f)** .... the water again.
On day three, Moby-Dick hits the *Pequod* with his head. Ahab's harpoon hits the white whale. But the harpoon rope goes **g)** .... Ahab's body, and pulls him **h)** .... into the sea. So he dies.

The *Pequod* goes **i)** ...., and everyone on her dies, too. But Ishmael jumps **j)** .... the ocean. He swims over **k)** .... Queequeg's coffin, and gets on it.
Two days later, the *Rachel* is sailing **l)** .... when Captain Gardiner sees Ishmael on the coffin. He takes the young sailor on board. Then the *Rachel* sails **m)** .... the ocean, back **n)** .... America.

DOMINOES Your Choice

Read *Dominoes* for pleasure, or to develop language skills. It's your choice.

Each *Domino* reader includes:
- a good story to enjoy
- integrated activities to develop reading skills and increase vocabulary
- task-based projects – perfect for CEFR portfolios
- contextualized grammar activities

Each *Domino* pack contains a reader, plus a MultiROM with:
- an excitingly dramatized audio recording of the story
- interactive games to improve skills

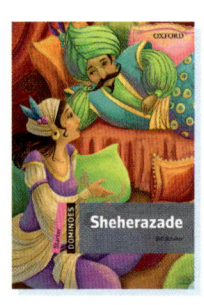

Sheherazade
Bill Bowler

King Shahriyar cannot trust women. Every afternoon he marries a wife, but the next morning he always kills her. One day, the Vizier cannot find any more wives for the King. What can he do?
'*I* can be Shahriyar's new wife!' says Sheherazade, his older daughter. 'God willing I can stay alive, and help the women of our country.'
But how can Sheherazade stay alive for a thousand and one nights? And does Shahriyar learn to trust women again in the end? This famous 'story of stories' has the answers.

Heidi
Johanna Spyri

'I'm not going with you, Aunt Dete!' Heidi cries.
'Oh yes, you are!' Dete answers.
Heidi loves her home in the Swiss mountains, her grandfather, and her friend Peter, the goatherd. So when Aunt Dete takes her away to Frankfurt, she doesn't leave happily.
In Frankfurt, Heidi is soon good friends with Clara Sesemann, a rich but very ill girl in a wheelchair.
But how can Heidi live without the mountains? And what can she do about Fräulein Rottenmeier, the Sesemanns' unfriendly housekeeper?

	CEFR	Cambridge Exams	IELTS	TOEFL iBT	TOEIC
Level 3	B1	PET	4.0	57–86	550
Level 2	A2–B1	KET-PET	3.0–4.0	–	390
Level 1	A1–A2	YLE Flyers/KET	3.0	–	225
Starter & Quick Starter	A1	YLE Movers	1.0–2.0	–	–

You can find details and a full list of books and teachers' resources on our website: www.oup.com/elt/gradedreaders